Alfred's Basic Piano Library

Chord Approach

A PIANO METHOD FOR THE LATER BEGINNER

Technic Book
LEVEL 1

FOREWORD

The Technic Books of Alfred's Basic CHORD APPROACH for piano are precisely coordinated with the LESSON BOOKS, THEORY BOOKS and SOLO BOOKS. The exercises in this book offer much more than the development of technical skill. They reinforce every principle introduced in the Lesson Books. They give additional drill in reading and playing melodic and harmonic intervals and chords. They improve musicianship, provide rhythm drills, and develop skill in coordination between the hands.

After a considerable amount of testing, new drills have been introduced at strategic places that give the student the opportunity to move up and down the keyboard, changing hand positions on each pattern or chord. This is helpful in overcoming the problem that often results when students become "locked" into a single hand position for a prolonged period. Students using these exercises have shown a better grasp of reading by intervals.

There are 14 groups of exercises in this book, plus one additional set for use away from the piano. Each group has just 4 exercises (A, B, C, D). The instructions at the beginning of each group of exercises show exactly where each group is to be introduced as the student moves through the corresponding Lesson Book.

CONTENTS

NOTE TO TEACHERS: For students to play the piano comfortably and correctly it is necessary that they develop good control of the fingers, hand, and arm. This involves constant attention to rounded fingers, relaxed wrists and arms, good posture at the keyboard, and all the vital elements with which you, as a professional piano instructor, are so abundantly familiar. Cautions and admonitions about these details are omitted from the music in this book, since they only clutter the page, and cannot, in any event, enforce themselves. Their absence should in no way indicate that the authors do not wish them properly emphasized. The amount of emphasis necessary will vary from student to student, and in this respect no book can replace the judgment and sensibilities of a fine teacher.

Group 1

Begin GROUP 1 EXERCISES when you are assigned page 16 in Alfred's CHORD APPROACH, Lesson Book 1.

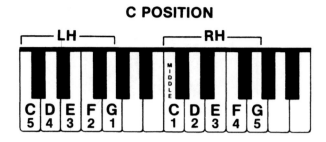

A. 2NDS IN PAIRS

Separate the pairs by lifting loosely from the wrist at the end of each slur.

Moderately slow to Moderately fast

B. 2NDS IN GROUPS OF THREE

Separate the groups of three by lifting from the wrist at the end of each slur.

Moderately slow to Moderately fast

C. SKILL DRILL

This exercise will improve your technic and your reading skill.

Practice each hand slowly at first. Later play more rapidly.

RH *legato*

LH *legato*

D. 2NDS IN FOUR HAND POSITIONS

Begin with RH 1 on C.

Move the hand position ONE KEY TO THE RIGHT for each of the following measures!

Moderately slow

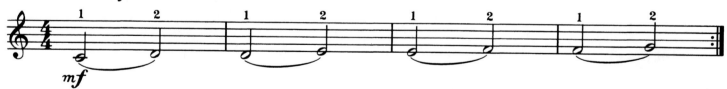

Begin with LH 1 on G.

Move the hand position ONE KEY TO THE LEFT for each of the following measures!

Play exercise D again, using the fingering 2 3 for each pair of 2nds.

IMPORTANT! See page 30 for exercises (A & B) you can practice AWAY FROM THE PIANO!

Group 2

Begin GROUP 2 EXERCISES when you are assigned *JOIN THE FUN* (page 19).

A. 3RDS IN PAIRS

Use "wrist lifts" between pairs.

Moderately slow to Moderately fast

* *f-p* means play *f* the first time, *p* the second time.

B. 3RDS IN GROUPS OF THREE

Use "wrist lifts" at the end of each slur.

Moderately slow to Moderately fast

* *mf-p* means play *mf* the first time, *p* the second time.

C. SKILL DRILL

Play each hand slowly at first. Gradually increase speed.

D. 3RDS IN CHANGING HAND POSITIONS

The hand position changes on each third.

After beginning with the RH thumb on C, move the hand ONE KEY TO THE RIGHT for each of the following measures. You need only to read the notes played with the thumb.

Moderately slow

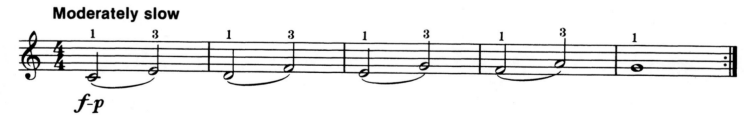

After beginning with the LH thumb on G, move the hand ONE KEY TO THE LEFT for each of the following measures.

IMPORTANT! Play exercise D again, using the fingering 2 4 for each pair of 3rds.

Group 3

Begin GROUP 3 EXERCISES with page 21.

A. MELODIC & HARMONIC 2NDS

Moderately slow to Moderately fast

B. MELODIC & HARMONIC 3RDS

Moderately slow to Moderately fast

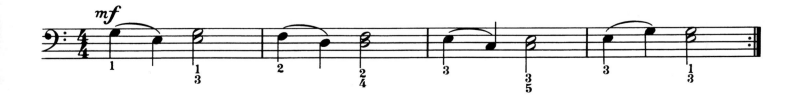

C. MOVING UP & DOWN THE KEYBOARD IN 2NDS

The hand position changes on each 2nd. After playing the first 2nd, simply move the 2nds up or down to the neighboring 2nd, as the notes move up or down the staff. You need only to read the notes played with the thumb.

Moderately slow

Repeat exercise C, playing each 2nd with the 2nd & 3rd fingers.

D. MOVING UP & DOWN THE KEYBOARD IN 3RDS

The hand position changes on each 3rd. After playing the first 3rd, simply move the 3rds up or down to the neighboring 3rd, as the notes move up or down the staff. You need only to read the notes played with the thumb.

Moderately slow

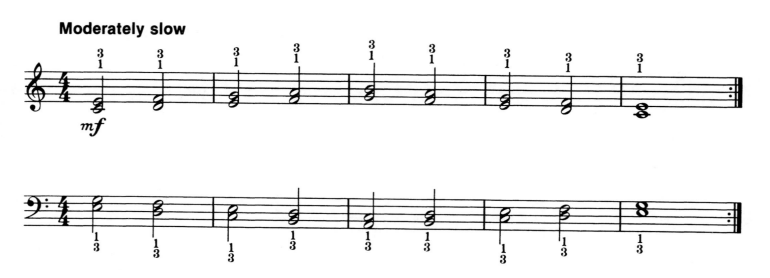

Repeat exercise D, playing each 3rd with the 2nd & 4th fingers.

Group 4

Assign A & B from GROUP 4 with page 22, C & D with page 23.

A. 4THS IN PAIRS

Moderately slow to Moderately fast

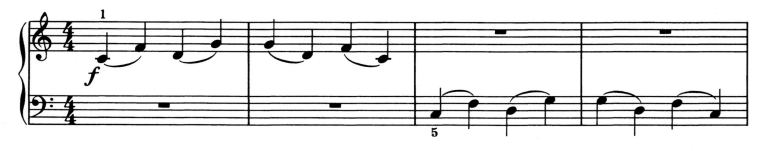

B. 4THS IN GROUPS OF THREE

Moderately slow to Moderately fast

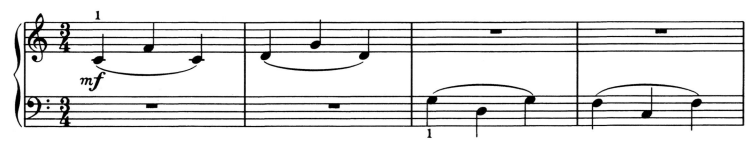

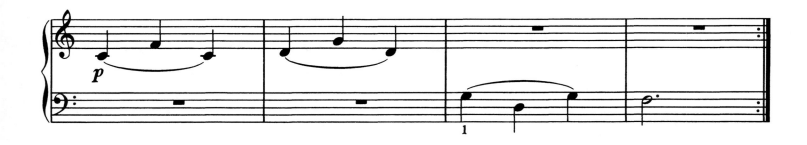

C. 5THS IN PAIRS
(Add when you reach page 23.)

Moderately slow to Moderately fast

D. MELODIC 2NDS, 3RDS, 4THS & 5THS
(Add when you reach page 23.)

Play with hands separate at first, then together.

Moderately slow to Moderately fast

IMPORTANT! See page 31 for another exercise (C) you can practice AWAY FROM THE PIANO!

Group 5

Begin GROUP 5 EXERCISES with page 24.

A. MELODIC & HARMONIC 4THS & 5THS

Moderately slow to Moderately fast

B. HARMONIC 2NDS, 3RDS, 4THS & 5THS

Moderately slow to Moderately fast

C. MOVING UP & DOWN IN 4THS

The hand position changes on each 4th.
After playing the first 4th, simply move up or down to the neighboring 4th, as the notes indicate.
You need only to read the notes played with the thumb.

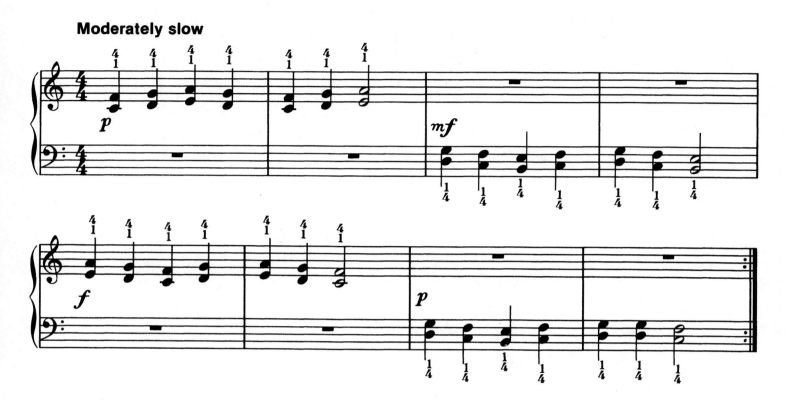

Repeat exercise C, playing each 4th with the 2nd & 5th fingers.

D. MOVING UP & DOWN IN 5THS

The hand position changes on each 5th.
Move up or down the keyboard, as the notes move up or down the staff.
You need only to read the notes played with the thumb.

IMPORTANT! See page 31 for another exercise (D) you can practice AWAY FROM THE PIANO!

Group 6

Begin GROUP 6 EXERCISES with page 26.

A. CHORD BUILDER

C major chords for LH & RH.

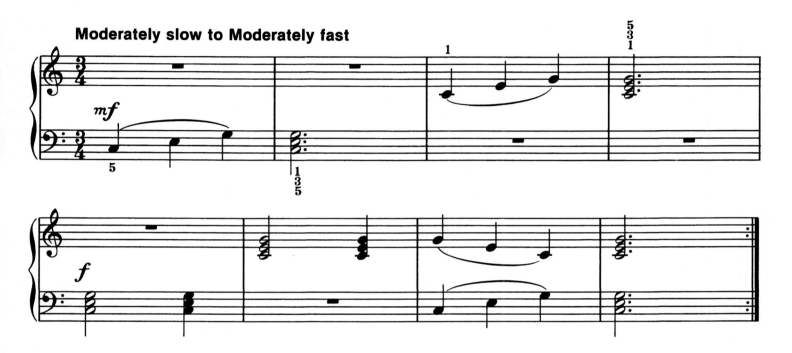

B. MELODIES & CHORDS

Bring the melody out. Play the chords softly.

RH melody, LH chords.

LH melody, RH chords.

C. SKILL BUILDER WITH MELODY & CHORDS

Moderately slow to Moderately fast

D. MOVING UP & DOWN WITH CHORDS

The hand position changes on each chord. Move to neighboring white keys.
You need only to read the notes played with the thumb.

Moderately slow

Group 7

Begin GROUP 7 EXERCISES with page 30.

A. BUILDING C MAJOR & G⁷ CHORDS

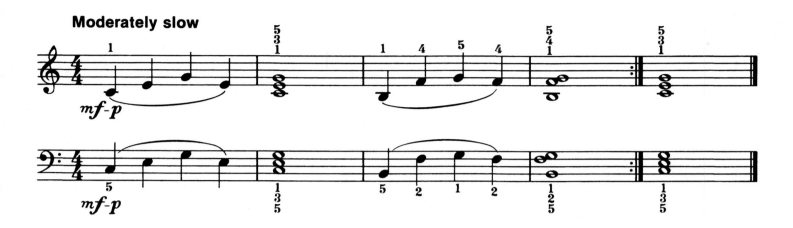

B. CLIMBING CHORDS

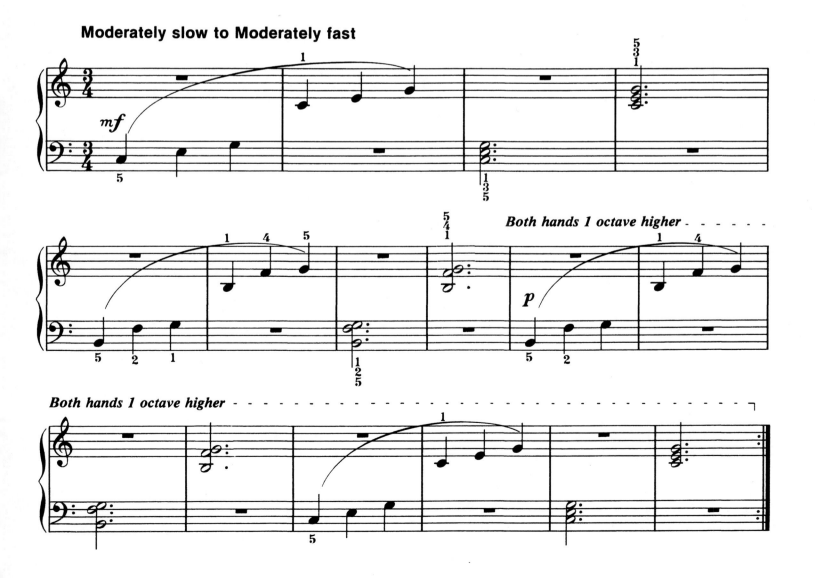

C. CROSS-OVERS

Moderately slow to Moderately fast

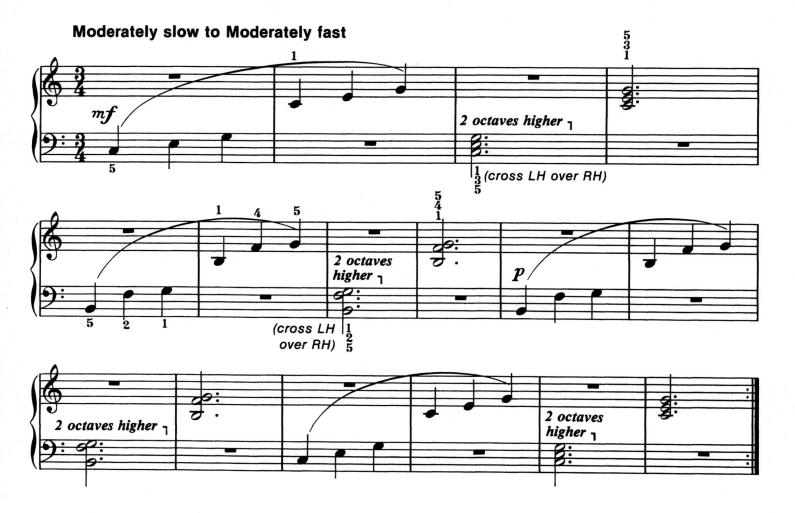

D. LEGATO MELODIES, "AFTER-BEAT" CHORDS

In this exercise, the melodies are played on the main beats of the measure (the 1st and 3rd counts). The chords are played on the "after-beats" (the 2nd and 4th counts).

Moderately slow to Moderately fast

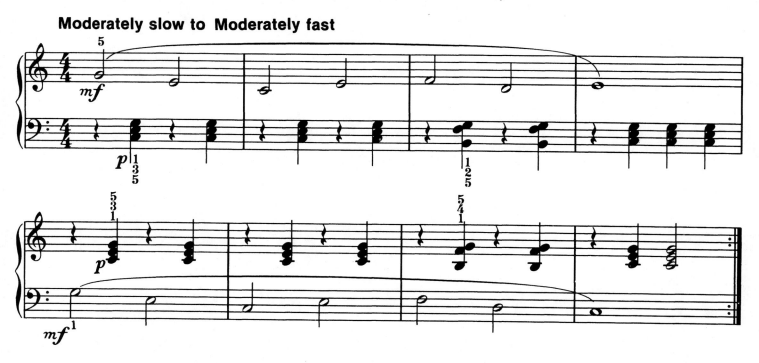

Group 8

Begin GROUP 8 EXERCISES with page 36.

A. BUILDING LH C MAJOR, F MAJOR & G⁷ CHORDS

Moderately slow

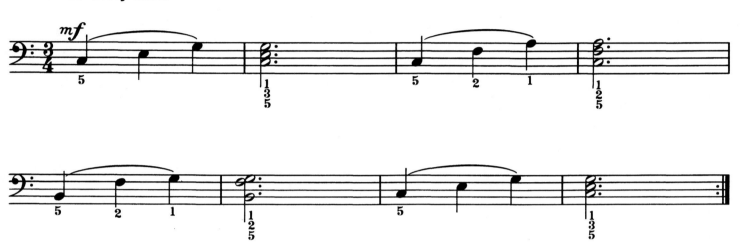

B. BUILDING RH C MAJOR, F MAJOR & G⁷ CHORDS

Moderately slow

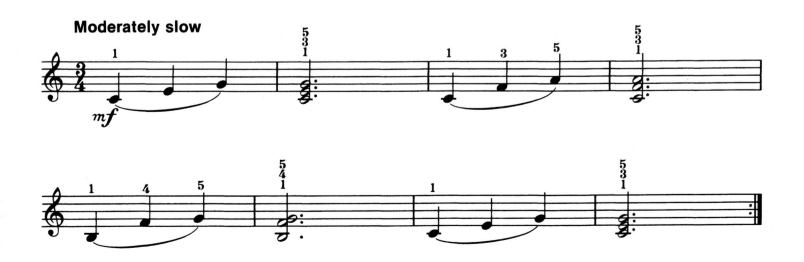

C. SKILL BUILDER WITH CHORD NOTES

Moderately slow to Moderately fast

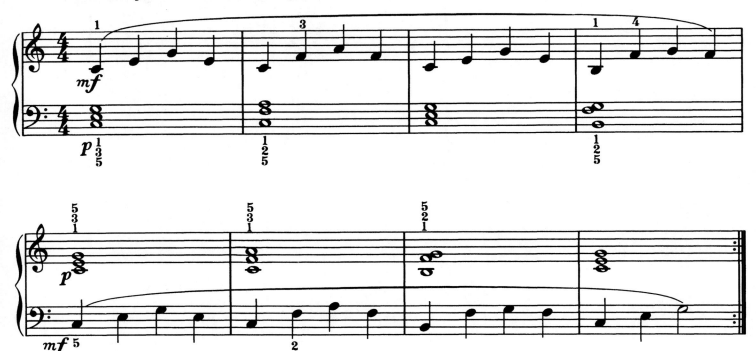

D. "ON-BEAT" & "AFTER-BEAT" CHORDS

Moderately slow to Moderately fast

BOTH HANDS 1 octave higher 2nd time

Group 9

Begin GROUP 9 EXERCISES with page 38.

G POSITION

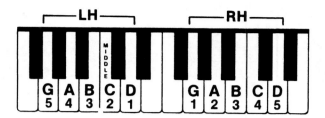

A. MELODIC & HARMONIC INTERVALS IN G POSITION

Play hands separately first, then together.

Moderately slow

B. HARMONIC WALTZ STUDY IN G POSITION

Moderately slow

C. SKILL BUILDER IN G POSITION

Play hands separately first, then together.

Moderately slow to Moderately fast

D. MOVING UP & DOWN IN 3RDS & 5THS

The hand position changes on each interval.

Harmonic 3rds. Play hands separately, then together.
You need only to read the notes played with the thumb.

Moderately slow to Moderately fast

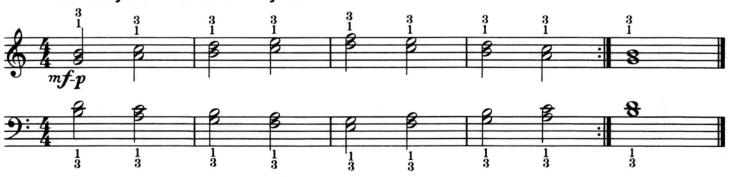

Harmonic 5ths. Play hands separately, then together.

Group 10

Assign A, B & C from GROUP 10 with page 44, D with page 45.

A. BUILDING G MAJOR & D⁷ CHORDS

Carefully observe *crescendos* and *diminuendos.*

Moderately slow to Moderately fast

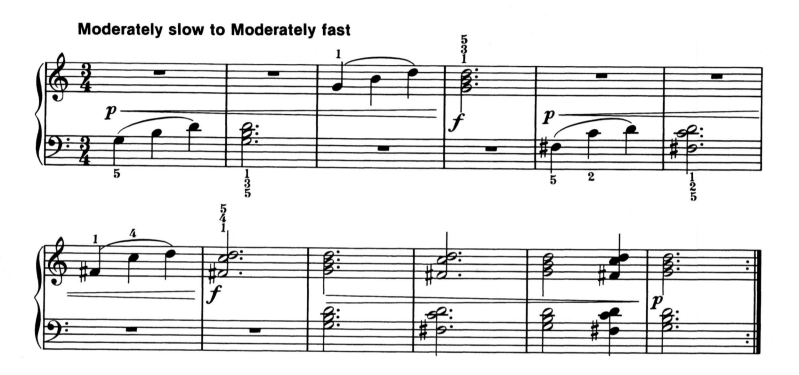

B. RH SKILL BUILDER WITH LH CHORDS

Moderately slow to Moderately fast

C. LH Skill Builder with RH Chords

Moderately slow to Moderately fast

D. Chord Cross-overs, with Pedal

(Add with page 45.)

Notice how much sound you can build with the pedal sustaining the chords.
In the 1st line, play each chord just a little louder than the one before.
In the 2nd line, play each chord a little softer.

Moderately slow

Group 11

Begin GROUP 11 EXERCISES with page 48.

A. RH G, C & D⁷ CHORDS, BROKEN & BLOCKED

Moderately slow to Moderately fast

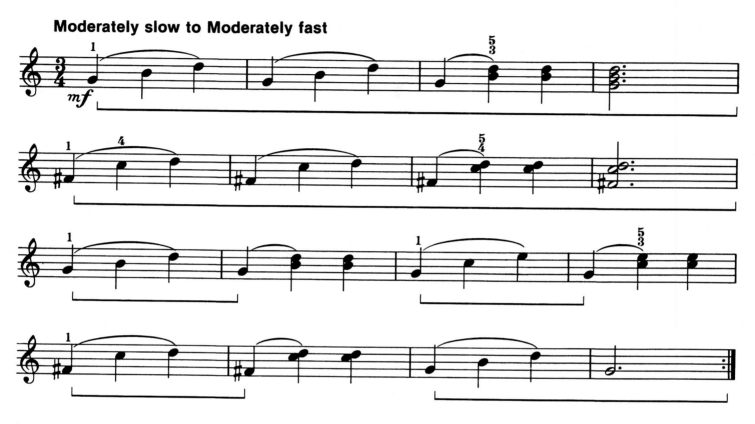

B. LH G, C & D⁷ CHORDS, BROKEN & BLOCKED

Moderately slow to Moderately fast

C. MORE CLIMBING CHORDS

Moderately slow to Moderately fast

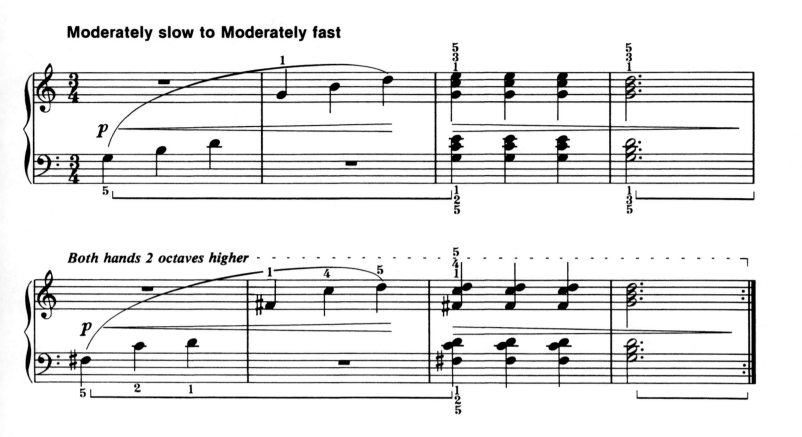

D. MORE "ON-BEAT" & "AFTER-BEAT" CHORDS

Moderately slow to Moderately fast

BOTH HANDS 1 octave higher 2nd time

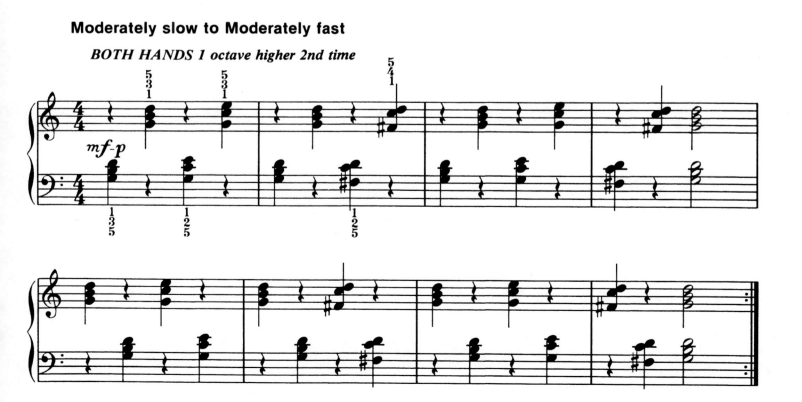

Group 12

Assign A & B from GROUP 12 with page 50,
C with page 52, and D with page 53.

MIDDLE C POSITION

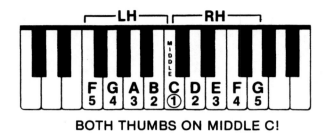

BOTH THUMBS ON MIDDLE C!

A. MIDDLE C SKILL DRILL NO. 1

Moderately slow to Moderately fast

B. MIDDLE C SKILL DRILL NO. 2

Moderately slow to Moderately fast

C. THEME IN MIDDLE C POSITION

(Add with page 52.)

Moderately slow to Moderately fast

D. VARIATION ON THE SAME THEME, WITH EIGHTH NOTES

(Add after page 53.)

Moderately slow to Moderately fast

Group 13

Assign A from GROUP 13 with page 56, B & C with page 57, and D with page 58.

A. SKILL DRILL IN MIDDLE C & C POSITIONS

Moderately slow to Moderately fast

B. BLUE ETUDE IN G POSITION

(Add with page 57.)

Moderately slow

C. BLUE ETUDE IN C POSITION

Slow

D. BOOGIE IN C & G POSITIONS

(Add with page 58.)

Moderately slow to Moderately fast

C POSITION

G POSITION

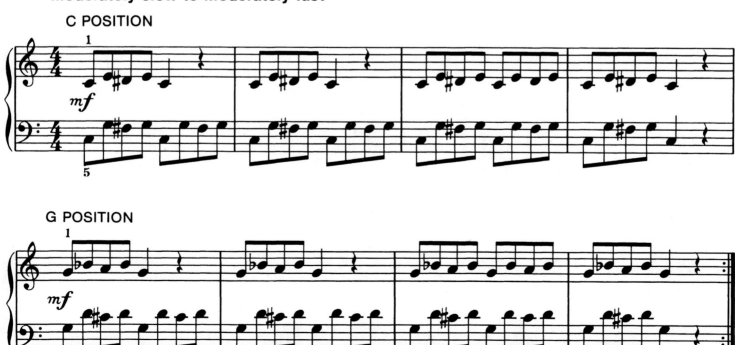

Group 14—Review

Assign GROUP 15 at the END of LESSON BOOK 1.

A. INTERVALS IN C POSITION

Moderately slow to Moderately fast

MELODIC INTERVALS

HARMONIC INTERVALS

B. CHORDS IN C POSITION

Moderately slow to Moderately fast

Both hands 1 octave higher 2nd time

C. INTERVALS IN G POSITION

Moderately slow to Moderately fast

MELODIC INTERVALS

HARMONIC INTERVALS

D. CHORDS IN G POSITION

Moderately slow to Moderately fast

Both hands 1 octave higher 2nd time

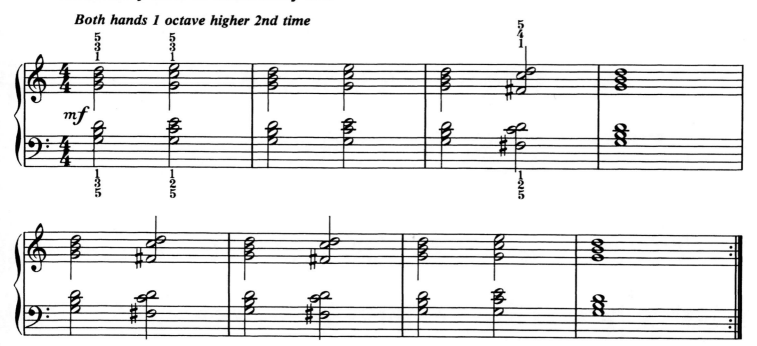

Table-Top Tricks

These are exercises you can do AWAY FROM THE PIANO.

When you are in a waiting room or riding in a car, or when you are anywhere away from your piano, you need not be bored or waste valuable time! You can improve you technic by practicing warm-ups while you wait.

The FUN of these warm-ups is that they are CHALLENGING! You may even laugh at how slowly some fingers respond at first, but later you will master all of these tricks, and they will make your playing much easier! If a table-top is not available, you may use a book or any other flat surface.

Begin each exercise as follows:

Place the hand *lightly* on the table.
Imagine you are in C POSITION, with the fingers on neighboring keys: C D E F G.
Let the wrist also rest lightly on the table-top.
Play the exercise, tapping each indicated finger very lightly. Take care not to
    press into the table-top.

VERY IMPORTANT! *All fingers that are not playing must rest on the surface at all times!*

A. REPEATING FINGERS
(Begin ANYTIME!)

B. FOR FINGER INDEPENDENCE
(Begin ANYTIME!)

C. MELODIC INTERVALS
(Begin after page 23.)

D. HARMONIC INTERVALS
(Begin after page 24.)

Make up some more exercises of your own.